42 MILES FROM OSMOTHERLEY TO RAVENSCAR

AN
ESSENTIAL GUIDE TO
HELP <u>YOU</u> COMPLETE
THE
LYKE WAKE WALK

BY
BRIAN G SMAILES

BRIAN SMAILES -

Has completed 31 crossings of the Lyke Wake Walk. These include one Lyke Wake run, one double crossing and four continuous crossings, the latter completed in June 1994. This achievement took 70 hours 50 minutes and overtook the 1968 record of 78 hours.

Most of the walks have raised sponsorship. The first crossing was in 1970, with regular crossings since in varying conditions completed in the last 10 years.

In completing this walk whether once or on four continuous crossings thanks must go to the support teams. Without their help much of his success and sponsorship raised would not have been possible.

CONTENTS

Lyke Wake Walk Ode   3

Introduction   4

Pre Walk Preparation   5

Equipment Selection   7

The Route   12

On Route Encounters   22

Support Team   27

Support Party Route   29

Post Walk   31

Lyke Wake Trivia Questions   32

Useful Information   33

Lyke Wake Trivia Answers   37

Lyke Wake Tale   38

PLATES

SCARTH WOOD MOOR   1

VIEW FROM CARLTON BANK   2

PEATBOG   3

PEATBOG   4

CHECKPOINT 4 WITH TUMULUS   5

OPEN MOORLAND   6

WHEELDALE BECK   7

NORTH YORK MOORS RAILWAY CROSSING   8

ELLERBECK, CHECKPOINT 5   9

LILLA CROSS ON LILLA HOWE   10

LYKE WAKE ODE

Now let me tell you a little tale,
Of Brian and his Lyke Wake trail,
He'll ramble on at every turn,
Of all the wonders you will learn,
How you will become self-sufficient and true,
How you'll laugh till you turn blue,
(From cold, that is, thought it won't be mentioned
Of course, this lapse was well-intentioned!)
He'll tell you too, of all the great sights,
Despite the fact it'll be pitch black nights,
And as for the hills (mountains) you will climb,
Well listen to Brian, and they're so small, it'll take no time,
The fact that on this great trek,
Rain, hail, snow and storms have known to wreck,
Is to Brian a minor incident,
All a part of what the Lyke Wake meant,
-Like boils and blisters on your feet,
Your aching backs, faces like beets,
Your upset tums, (have you had the food!)
Your knees that collapse,
As you crawl the final laps!
So just remember when you see his smiling face,
His shining eyes, as his pulses race,
His confident air, his enthusiastic words,
- This walk is especially for ....!!!

Diane Roberts

INTRODUCTION

The Lyke Wake Walk is a 42 mile crossing of the North Yorkshire moors. Official starting point is the Lyke Wake stone just past the reservoir at Osmotherley and finishing at the Lyke Wake stone on Beacon Howes at Ravenscar.

This crossing is generally considered a hard walk and a challenge to most people. There are seven sections with checkpoints between. Each section presents a different challenge. The first two sections of the walk run concurrently with the Cleveland Way before the Lyke Wake turns off East along a disused railway track.

Thousands of people each year attempt this challenge. Those people who prepare beforehand usually succeed, those who do not prepare, suffer on route. This booklet is a plain speaking guide which should help every one particularly the novice walker who may be either accepting a challenge or doing the walk as a "one off" for charity sponsorship. The walk although 42 miles of pure sweat and toil can be as easy or as hard as you make it.

All references to places and roads are taken from the ordnance survey map of the North Yorkshire moors - tourist version No.2 and it is strongly recommended, this map is used to complement this guide. Read on:-

The Lyke Wake Club, the North York Moors National Park Authority, and the author are strongly opposed to large parties (10 or more) undertaking the Lyke/Wake Walk. Parties should be kept small to help avoid damage to the route.

When preparing for this walk there are a number of points to consider. Fitness helps a lot when attempting the crossing. Past experience has shown me that people who do some type of fitness training in preparation for this walk usually succeed. Those people who get in a car and drive from A to B and do nothing energetic are more likely to struggle.

After taking hundreds of people across these moors over many years and discussing their training with them I have reached the following conclusion. This may help you decide which type of training to do.

Without a doubt the best training for this walk is jogging. Generally up to 7 miles maximum in one run after building up gradually would be enough over a period of time.

Next in fitness training is walking itself. Ideally this should be done regularly and gradually at least over a two month period. Start with a short walk and increase over time to a 25 mile walk the week before the event. This should prepare you adequately by toning up your leg muscles as well as bedding your new boots in.

Other ways to help you get fit are cycling, swimming, keep fit sessions and other types of workouts.

Suitable equipment is another factor which helps. This need not be expensive but should be adequate for the job in hand. Equipment will be discussed in the next chapter in more detail.

Training in the use of a compass and map reading would be an advantage, particularly if you are doing the walk on your own or in a small group with no experienced guide or support team.

Throughout the walk there are numerous paths, sheep tracks and farmers paths which the unexperienced walker could quite easily wander along. Many of the tracks run parallel for a time then gradually lead off in different directions, therefore basic training in compass use would help, especially in the event of bad weather.

Food of the right type to give energy and goodness to the body both before and during the walk is essential. Generally food containing a high level of carbohydrates consumed the week before the walk and while walking would help in producing energy. High energy food such as rice, pasta, potato, banana and milk will all help to build up your energy reserves and enable you to carry on when the going gets tough.

While walking you may find that high energy carbohydrate tablet / sweets or barley sugar will help you maintain a constant supply of energy. These are obtainable from many shops.

Now you have prepared adequately and are fit to tackle this arduous course, the next chapter looks at the equipment you need to complement your body preparation.

EQUIPMENT SELECTION

There is a vast amount of equipment you could use for this type of event costing from pence to pounds. The following list has been compiled from walkers comments and from what is reasonable for a person to carry on this particular walk. The equipment should not prove too expensive and indeed many walkers will already have most of the items on this list. This is only a suggested list and you may wish to vary it to suit your individual requirements.

1. Ordnance survey map of North Yorkshire moors - tourist version No.2.
2. Walking boots or fell boots (spare laces?)
3. Stockings / socks at least three pair.
4. Gloves.
5. Woollen hat.
6. Thin warm jumpers (in layers)
7. Loose fitting trousers / walking trousers - not jeans.
8. Cagoul / anorak / overtrousers (waterproof)
9. Complete spare change of clothes.
10. Extra jumper for cold weather.
11. A pair of soft shoes / trainers for before and after the walk and to be carried in case of problems with boots while walking.
12. Basic first aid kit including plasters for blisters and vaseline for chafing.
13. Small rucksack.
14. Compass.
15. Survival bag.
16. Torch with spare batteries.
17. Whistle.
18. Talcum powder for feet.
19. 20p coin for telephone in case of emergency.
20. Note paper / pencil.
21. Toilet paper.
22. Plastic drinks bottle not more than 1 litre. You have to carry it 42 miles.

23. Glucose tablets / sweets.
24. Camera.

When considering your equipment it is advisable to travel to the start in some comfortable trainers or shoes then change into your boots at the start of the walk. This means you will only have your boots on for the 12 - 19 hours that it would normally take you to complete the crossing.

A common problem with this walk is upper leg muscle stiffness. Many people are accustomed to wearing light shoes on their feet. They then put on a pair of heavy boots and expect to walk 42 miles without the necessary training to tone and build up the upper leg muscles. Result is muscles stiffen and eventually seize. Many people have this problem and have to either drop out on route or be closely supported to the nearest check point, so beware!

I was once give a useful tip regarding boots and the avoidance of blisters - boots need to be big enough to fit comfortably but not too big so your feet move around inside while walking. Remember to fit the boots with suitable socks before buying.

Sprinkle a liberal quantity of talcum powder on your feet and in the socks. Put talcum powder into your boots and on the out sides of your socks, then put your boots on making sure your feet fit snuggly into them. This method has helped many people to keep their feet not only dry and fresh throughout but more importantly blister free after 42 miles.

Remember to cut your toe nails short before you leave home so you don't get any undue pressure on your toes while walking.

Walking in jeans is unadvisable for two reasons 1) When jeans get wet they are liable to rub and chafe the skin to the point where you can be extremely sore. 2) Wet jeans draw the body heat away which could leave you colder instead of warmer and may result in hypothermia.

Two extremely useful items are a pair of gloves and a woollen hat. Most heat is lost through the back of the head therefore it is prudent to carry a hat or balaclava to help retain your body heat especially in times of cold and wet weather. Because heat is also lost quickly from your extremities, gloves are a useful item to carry to help towards overall protection.

Plate 1

Scarth Wood Moor at the begining of the Lyke Wake Walk
The Hill in the background is Carlton Bank just before 1st checkpoint.
Coalmire Plantation is in the centre.

Plate 2

Near Triangulation pillar on Carlton Bank the hill in the background is
cringle moor showing the clear path up to the top. To the left on the
hill is the alternative route.

THE ROUTE

As stated earlier the walk is divided into seven sections starting at the Lyke Wake Stone near Osmotherley. Time for this first section is approximately two hours based on a total walking time of 13 hours not including stops at checkpoints. The distance is 6 miles.

Proceed up the hill from the Lyke Wake Stone then turn right and easterly (Plate 1) along the top and continue for a short distance until the path meets the metalled road. Cross the road following the path and signs through the forest and down the hill. At the bottom take your second turning right. Proceed until you arrive at a stile with a field beyond. Cross the field and stream below then proceed up the metalled road to the telephone box at Huthwaite Green. Go through the gate and you meet the challenge for this section half a mile further on this track.

A set of steps rises steeply. These are at various heights and lengths. Because of the awkward and uneven step and the total number together with the height climbed, most walkers feel temporarily exhausted on reaching the top. At the time of writing this book, work is starting on the laying of stone steps which hopefully will benefit the walker and help combat path erosion.

After completing the steps challenge you leave the tree line with the wind probably getting stronger as you start the steady climb up live moor on newly laid path. This eventually leads up to the triangulation pillar on Carlton bank. (Plate 2) Height climbed is 1338 FT. Care needs to be taken especially on this first section while the body adapts to the conditions and changing temperature. More importantly can be the differences in weather from no wind at the start to gale force winds at the summit on Carlton Bank with low cloud and extreme cold. The glider base at the top is a useful landmark but keep on the path along the edge to the left up to the triangulation pillar. Turn right and head down a path which is steep and rocky in places to arrive at check point one, entrance to Carlton Bank glider club at the road crossing.

Section two of the walk takes approximately one and a half hours and is four miles long. After leaving checkpoint one there are two directions you can take. The first takes you up a straight forward path which is very steep but leads you directly to the top of the hill named Drake Howe on Cringle moor. Once at the top there are excellent views up to 60 miles on a clear day. Continue along the path on the top and down at the far side before proceeding along the right side of the forest known as Broughton Plantation.

The alternative route that can be used particularly in bad weather is a path around the left side of the hill. This path is undulating with some water and springs appearing as you proceed around the side of the hill. Access is gained through a gate at the foot of the hill. Whichever route you choose you will arrive at Broughton Plantation with a path along the right side.

On arriving at the forest go down a short steep ditch or dyke and back up the other side where the forest begins. Most walkers go this way though some prefer to traverse along the high, exposed peaks on your right. The path along the forest side can be very wet and muddy with many stones interspersed along the route. Because there is a stone wall on one side and forest on the other this stretch is generally quite sheltered. This section is usually considered a good toilet stop but these diminish as the walk progresses. Toilet stops are generally few and far between.

Just before arriving at checkpoint 2 you decend the hill called Hasty Bank where the path widens. Here you will see a seat on your right side. Bear right at the seat after reading the inscription on it and go down the stone steps at the side of the wall to checkpoint 2 on Clay Bank road.

Section 3 is the longest section and takes approximately 3 hours for this 10 mile route. It starts with a step climb up the hill on Urra Moor to Botton Head which is the highest point on the whole walk, 1490 FT. On the top the path is seen to be winding into the distance.

Plate 3

Typical conditions encountered in peat bog.

Plate 4

That sinking feeling on route to checkpoint 4

Following this path leads you to the old railway line. When you see the railway line, bear right off the Cleveland Way and go along a short path leading up to the old railway line at a point called Bloworth Crossing, 1274 FT.

This railway track is the main challenge in this section. Continue in an easterly direction for 2.5 miles. Eventually you will see a mound of lime on your left side. Walk a further two miles. Just past Blakey Gill there is a short path off on your left up to the Lion Inn. Turn left here and head for Ralph Crosses 'T' Junction where checkpoint 3 at Rosedale Head awaits you.

When walking on the old railway line it can be very windy as the wind sweeps up the valley and over the embankments. It would be advisable to carry suitable wind/waterproof clothing while walking on this exposed track.

Prepare at checkpoint 3 for wet feet because the challenge in this next section is the peat bogs. (Plate3) This 5 mile section usually takes around 2 hours to complete but wet or dry conditions can affect your travelling time by quite a lot. Turn right from Ralph Crosses and walk along the road towards Rosedale Abbey for nearly 2 miles. This road is at least reasonably flat so gives the legs some relief although there is a path that runs across moorland from Ralph Crosses to arrive at the same point where you need to turn off the road.

When you leave the road turn left at the highest point of the surrounding land which is after the road on your left. This road leads to Danley approximately 5.5 miles to the North.

Cross the platform bridge over the roadside dyke on to a well worn path. This can be difficult to find as you leave the road. Once over the brow of the hill you will be walking on thick peat. When dry you tend to bounce across, when wet you sink into it. (Plate 4) There are natural springs which come to the surface so the ground is very wet in parts with reed beds and surface water or black wet peat where you can sink in sometimes when you least expect it. The path from leaving the road to checkpoint 4 at Shunner Howe is a direct straight line so not hard to follow except in fog or snow. (Plate 5)

Experience has shown that to travel fairly light over this short section if weather conditions permit, would help. The reason for this is because there are a number of dykes or ditches that you must cross. These are often full of water or unstable peat. To enable you to pass from one side to the other easier, leave heavy rucksacks and equipment with the back up team but retain waterproof and spare warm clothing with you. I must emphasise that this should only be done in times of good weather and with a reliable support team to meet you at checkpoint 4.

The next section is approximately 9 miles and takes around 2 hours 20 minutes for this demanding stretch from Shunner Howe to Eller Beck on the Pickering to Whitby road. Many people say this section is more than 9 miles long. This is usually because they are often feeling stiff by this time and walking at a slower pace.

The challenge in this section is the steep ravine which the unsuspecting walker suddenly finds themselves at the top of. Before you arrive at the ravine you have, in parts, a difficult path to follow. When you leave Shunner Howe the path is quite well defined and can be wet and peaty for the first mile. Head for the high ground ahead called Blue Man i 'th' Moss in a generally easterly direction. Once on the top the path then becomes very rock strewn and difficult to navigate over as well as being hard to follow. (Plate 6)

Wheeldale Plantation is 0.5 mile to your left. You will see the forest as you proceed along the rocky path but bear right along the forest line keeping it at a distance. The path continues to have many rocks on it until you cross Wheeldale road and the terrain changes to more picturesque scenery. You proceed down the side of a farmers field that has been reclaimed from moorland. Here you cross the Roman road and see the steep ravine you need to decend. (Plate 7)

Cross the stepping stones and ascend the other side on a steady climb to Simon Howe. At this point you will see checkpoint 5 at Fylingdales with good views of all the surrounding area.

A long decent brings you to the railway line of the North Yorkshire moors railway. You may even see the steam train on its regular journey from Grosmont to Pickering. (Plate 8) Cross over and up the bank to checkpoint 5 at Eller Beck bridge. There is only 8 miles to complete now. It is advisable to consume food and drink quickly then continue before the legs become too stiff - Time wasting at this stage could be critical!

Section 5 takes you across the road which can be very busy. (Plate 9) Follow a path that leads along the side of Little Eller Beck stream and skirts around the military area of Fylingdales. The path will take you to Lilla Howe which is the smaller of the two mounds on the skyline in front of you.

After leaving Little Eller Beck stream to your left go up a man made stoney road along the North Western side of the military area to just before Lilla Howe. A short piece of sometimes boggy ground and you arrive at Lilla Howe. (Plate 10) At this point you have excellent views of the finish and surrounding area. The path takes you steadily downhill now but after 2 miles you meet the next challenge. You again find yourself at the top of another ravine with a steep decent and ascent which you need to make to overcome this final challenge. This is Jugger Howe ravine which is crossed at the bottom by a narrow` platform bridge. It has a steep ascent up the other side before it leads on to a gravel path then an old army road to checkpoint 6 which is Jugger Howes at 630 ft near the Flask Inn on the Whitby/Scarborough road.

You will probably find at this stage that it is better to continue on to the finish rather than stop here for refreshments and possibly seize up.

Cross the main A171 road and up a short, steep embankment on to Stony Marl moor then it is a straight path in a North Easterly direction for 2 miles to finish at the Lyke Wake Stone at Beacon Howes 871 ft. This will take approximately 30 minutes.

Celebrations are in order if you have enough energy otherwise take a well earned rest! If you have completed the walk within 24 hours you automatically become a member of the Lyke Wake Club (see Post Walk Section).

'C O N G R A T U L A T I O N S'

Plate 5
View from Checkpoint 4 looking back to the tumulus at the brow of the
hill.

Plate 6
Two Lyke Wake walkers on open moorland showing a path of mud and
stones on route.

Plate 7

View of the stepping stones over Wheeldale Beck with the path leading over the hills towards checkpoint 5.

ON ROUTE ENCOUNTERS

Throughout the walk there are numerous items of interest. I will describe these in order of passing.

When starting near Osmotherley you will see the Lyke Wake Stone which is an awesome momento of what lies ahead.

Through the forest soon after starting you may see deer, fox, numerous rabbits and grouse. These animals have been sighted on many occasions.

On Carlton Bank 5.5 miles into your journey there are excellent views from the top and along to the triangulation pillar. These include Bilsdale television booster mast which is a landmark to the South East. Middlesborough and the Cleveland area can also be seen clearly from the top.

Even more awe inspiring are the views from the top of Drake Howe on Cringle Moor. (Plate 2) At a height of 1427 FT the panoramic view is spectacular. On a clear day Penshaw monument near my home town of Sunderland can be seen over 60 miles away to the North.

Proceeding towards checkpoint 2 you will pass a wooden seat near the end of the forest section. This has an inscription on it which you should read then proceed with vigour to the checkpoint!

Along the railway line past Bloworth crossing there is a pile of limestone or chippings. Just past here is a turning to the left down into Westerdale Moor. This gives good viewing for those with time to spare and is in fact the old route of Lyke Wake Walk down into the valley and up Flat Howe to Ralph Crosses at Rosedale Head, checkpoint 3.

Near Ralph Crosses is an unusual boundary stone named White Cross but commonly known as Fat Betty which you will see on route to the bog section. It forms part of the line of boundary stones but is individually distinctive.

Water, Water everywhere! Depending on the conditions and time of year you may find yourself up to the knees in black slimey peat or bouncing over it as you walk. On this route to Shunner Howe you may still see the remains of a fir tree on your right side as you proceed to the checkpoint. This was a small tree when I first started my crossings many years ago. It grew quite large before being either partly cut down or diseased and now appears to have died. Only the lower trunk remains.

After passing several tumili on your right (Plate 5) you arrive at Shunner Howe, checkpoint 4. On route to Eller Beck you can actually see the radio beacon at the finish near Ravenscar. This sighting may give inspiration to those who may be 'struggling' at this stage.

A pleasant sight as you proceed is the scenery and the general area around the old Roman road. This leads quickly down to Wheeldale Beck. (Plate 7) Many people pause here for picnics and to bathe their feet in the beck near the stepping stones. A youth hostel nearby can make a good stopping off point for the night for those with time to spare.

When you make the long slow climb up towards the high ground and Simon Howe, 850 FT, you will see the new Fylingdales military area from the top. The old 'golf balls' were removed in May 1994. Checkpoint 5 at Eller Beck is another popular place for picnics near the bridge but beware of the busy road. (Plate 9)

Between checkpoints 5 & 6 is Lilla Howe. This is a raised earth mound on the hill and it supports a cross which is an early example of Christian Sculpture relating to Edwin, King of Northumbria in 633 AD. (Plate 10)

On reaching this point there are good views of Beacon Howes,

Scarborough and the sea. Grouse are often seen not only in this area but throughout the length of the walk.

Jugger Howe ravine is an intrepid sight from the top and sets a daunting task for any walker just before checkpoint 6 to traverse both sides of this steep and potentially dangerous ravine and have the energy left to complete the last 3 miles.

Eventually you arrive at the Lyke Wake Stone at Beacon Howes near Ravenscar. If you have enough energy, walk to your left of the radio beacon and look over the cliff. Good views of Robin Hoods Bay and the surrounding area can be seen from here.

Walkers may like to note that within 3 miles of the finish there are some local public houses including the Flask Inn, Raven Hall hotel and the Falcon Inn. The famous Smugglers Inn is only 0.5 mile South of Beacon Howes for those in need of urgent refreshment!

Plate 8
North York Moors railway with Lyke Wake path crossing over just
before checkpoint 5.

Plate 9
Looking back to Eller Beck, checkpoint 5 showing the car park, busy
road and walkers route in foreground.

Plate 10

Lilla Cross on Lilla Howe between checkpoint 5 and 6.

From this point the finish at Beacon Howes can usually be seen clearly.

Most people usually attempt this walk from Osmotherley to Ravenscar with a support team who will meet them at each checkpoint and provide food and drinks. It is important to remember that if you are a walker you should keep in mind the distance between each checkpoint and the approximate time to complete the section. Consider your physical and mental state as you progress to each checkpoint and the weather conditions. You should then be able to decide whether you can continue to the next checkpoint or retire honourably at the one you are at.

A good support team who give verbal encouragement as well as hot food and drinks are essential for all walkers. When arriving at a checkpoint walkers should not have to wait for food and drinks. These should be ready as the walkers arrive. Too long spent at a checkpoint will result in walkers feeling stiff and tired. As the walk progresses the time spent at a checkpoint becomes more critical as the body becomes stiffer.

Walkers should arrive at a checkpoint, be fed and watered and set off again within 15 minutes if possible.

A good safety precaution is for the backup team to operate a checking in system at each checkpoint. Walkers should report to their car or minibus driver at each checkpoint and be marked off on a walkers register. Taking this precaution should ensure no walker has gone astray between checkpoints.

All support teams must have adequate supply of first aid equipment particularly adhesive plasters. They should also carry sleeping bags for any possible hypothermia cases and torches with spare batteries for any emergency at night.

Support teams should have if possible one person who is familiar with the walk and understands the problems the walkers face in each section. There may be a need to go along the route to retrieve or assist a tired or injured walker. An emergency rucksack with the necessary equipment in should be ready. This pack should include some food and drink, note pad, pen, windproof, warm clothing and survival bag.

The success or failure of individuals or the whole group depends in some situations on how good the support team are overall and if they are at exactly the right place at the right time. This is sometimes a problem in thick fog! A good support team should have a responsible project leader who will have basic first aid skills and be a competant map reader.

From the car park, North for 2 miles to A172, turn right, after 2 miles turn right and South East through Carlton in Cleveland and up the hill a total of 6 miles.

CHECKPOINT 1 CARLTON BANK

Top of the hill with small signpost "CAFE" on left.

Continue on same road to B1257, at Chop Gate 9.3 miles, turn left and head North to Hasty Bank a further 2 miles.

CHECKPOINT 2 HASTY BANK

Lay by on both sides before the corner, (trees on left). Steps down side of forest.

Continue North from lay by and first turning right to Ingleby Greenhow 2 miles, and Battersby 1.5 miles and Kildale a further 2 miles all in a North Easterly direction. 1.5 miles after Kildale head South East to Westerdale 3.5 miles and a further 2.5 miles to second car park.

CHECKPOINT 3 RALPH CROSSES

Gravel car park on corner at the junction.

Head South East to Rosedale Abbey a distance of 5.5 miles, turn left at public house in village and head North East for 3 miles.

CHECKPOINT 4 HAMER HOUSE

Old pits or tumulus then a wide path on left. Grass area near road also a few stones from ruins of Hamer House

Continue North East for 6 miles to Egton Bridge and East for 1.5 miles to Grosmont, head East and then South East for 2 miles to A169, turn right and South for 4 miles to checkpoint 5.

CHECKPOINT 5 ELLER BECK

Lay by on right just above bridge.

Head back, North on same road towards Sleights and after 4.5 miles turn right and East to Littlebeck (1 mile). Continue East to join B1416 after 1 mile. Continue on this road and join A171. Turn right and head

South for 3 miles to checkpoint 6.

CHECKPOINT 6 JUGGER HOWES

1.5 miles past Flask Inn turn right into lay by on right at top of hill. Entrance from lay by to ruin of old army camp. Padlocked gate and stile there.

Continue on same road for 2 miles then turn left to Ravenscar. After 1 mile turn left at junction and head North West to finish at Beacon Howes.

FINISH POINT 7

Radio mast near Ravenscar and Lyke Wake Stone.

Having arrived at Ravenscar after completing 42 miles over peat bog, hill and dale you are now an automatic member of the Lyke Wake Club, provided you have completed the walk within 24 hours. To obtain the official badge and certificate you should write to the

> LYKE WAKE CLUB
> P.O. BOX 24
> NORTHALLERTON
> NORTH YORKSHIRE
> DL6 3HZ

Send a stamp addressed envelope for an up to date price list of badges and certificates etc, which you can obtain after completion.

You will probably find that having walked 42 miles often in cold and wet conditions you may experience problems while getting out of your transport upon arriving home. A hot bath with some bath salts added should help the body to recover quicker.

LYKE WAKE WALK TRIVIA QUESTIONS

1. Name the inscription on the seat just before checkpoint 2
2. Name the distinctive stone near Ralph Crosses (check point 3)
3. Name the beck near the old Roman road
4. What do you expect to see on you left side as you proceed along the old railway line
5. Name the ravine you need to traverse 3 miles from Beacon Howe, Ravenscar
6. Which is the highest point of the Lyke Wake Walk
7. Between which 2 checkpoints is the main bog section
8. Name the only youth hostel you pass on your route
9. What would you expect to see at the start and the end of the walk
10. Where does the Cleveland Way turn off from the Lyke Wake Walk
11. Which section crosses the North York moors railway line
12. Name the mound on the hill where an early Christian cross stands
13. Name the location of the telephone box you pass on route
14. What is the grid reference of Hasty Bank (checkpoint 2)
15. In which section are the 'steps' challenge
16. Name the most common bird on North York moors.
17. Name the first forest or plantation you will go through on your journey

All answers can be found within this book
List of answers can be found on page 37

USEFUL INFORMATION

MILEAGE-OSMOTHERLEY TO RAVENSCAR

Checkpoints		Miles		Times
0-1	=	6	=	2 hours
1-2	=	4	=	1 hour 30 mins
2-3	=	10	=	3 hours
3-4	=	5	=	2 hours
4-5	=	9	=	2 hours 20 mins
5-6	=	6	=	1 hour 40 mins
6-F	=	2	=	30 mins

42 TOTAL

Based on an approximate walking time of 13 hours, not including breaks at checkpoints. Actual walking times vary depending on the number of walkers and the conditions at time of walk.

In Osmotherley and Ravenscar there are bed and breakfast houses. It is best to acquire the latest list from the National Park Office in Helmsley. On route there is Wheeldale Lodge Youth Hostel for those who prefer to do the walk over 2 days. In Ravenscar the village hall is available, contact Mrs Russell in Church Road, tel 870801.

The hills and valleys climbed amount to 5000 FT.

The last public telephone after leaving Osmotherley until you arrive at Ravenscar is at Huthwaite Green.

When attempting this challenging walk it is advisable to start around midnight while you are feeling fresh and finish around 4-6pm when you are exhausted but with daylight left. This is even more important during winter months when it gets dark earlier. Leave enough time to finish in the daylight allowing extra time at the end for varying weather and walking conditions.

Those people who are super fit can attempt the Lyke Wake race which is held in conjunction with the Osmotherley village games in July each year. Starting at Beacon Howes, Ravenscar, the normal route is followed right into Osmotherley rather than finishing at the Lyke Wake Stone. Times for the race are around 5-6 hours. Details from the Lyke Wake club.

The badge and certificate both have coffins on them to symbolise early Yorkshire folklore whereby people buried their dead in the mounds or tumulus we pass on route and indeed throughout these moors. They also remember a Lyke Wake dirge from the 17th century which was sung at funerals.

Weather conditions throughout the walk can vary considerably. A calm, still evening leaving Osmotherley can turn into gale force winds on the tops and torrential rain on route. In preparing yourself before the walk the best advice is to expect rain, cold and wet peat bogs. Anything better is a bonus!

At night, if you are lost but are warm and unhurt, find a sheltered area, in heather if possible. Put on warm clothing and keep well covered and out of the wind. Eat some food before waiting until daylight to establish your position and continue on your way or head for the nearest habitation or telephone. During this period, if at all possible contact your support party. Experience has shown that telephones, CB`s etc unless very powerful don`t work well in this hilly area. Expensive communication equipment will not take kindly to a 42 mile rucksack bumping.

DISTANCE TO NEAREST MAIN VILLAGES

START POINT	- OSMOTHERLEY	1 MILE
CHECKPOINT 1	- CARLTON IN CLEVELAND	1.25 MILE
CHECKPOINT 2	- GREAT BROUGHTON	2.9 MILE
CHECKPOINT 3	- CASTLETON	4 MILE
CHECKPOINT 4	- EGTON BRIDGE	5 MILE
CHECKPOINT 5	- PICKERING	10.5 MILE
CHECKPOINT 6	- WHITBY	10 MILE
BEACON HOWES	- RAVENSCAR	1 MILE

GRID REFERENCES AT MAIN WAY POINTS

START 469994
HUTHWAITE GREEN 493007
CHECKPOINT 1 523030
CHECKPOINT 2 573033
BLOWORTH CROSSING 616015
ROSEDALE HEAD 676019
TURN OFF ROAD TO BOG SECTION 698012
CHECKPOINT 4 744995
WHEELDALE BECK 812983
CHECKPOINT 5 857983
LILLA HOWE 889987
JUGGER HOWES RAVINE 930994
CHECKPOINT 6 945004
BEACON HOWES 970013

HEIGHTS CLIMBED ON ROUTE

LYKE WAKE STONE 670 FT
SCARTH WOOD MOOR 982 FT
LIVE MOOR 1025 FT
CARLTON BANK 1338 FT
CRINGLE MOOR 1427 FT
HASTY BANK 1384 FT
BOTTON HEAD 1490 FT
BLOWORTH CROSSING 1274 FT
ROSEDALE HEAD 1370 FT
LOOSE HOWE 1418 FT
SHUNNER HOWE 1065 FT
BLUE MAN I 'TH' MOSS 1043 FT
WHEELDALE LODGE 550 FT
ELLER BECK BRIDGE 564 FT
LILLA HOWE 959 FT
JUGGER HOWES 630 FT
BEACON HOWES 871 FT

LYKE WAKE TRIVIA ANSWERS

1. In memory of Robbie who died near here on Lyke Wake walk
2. Fat Betty or White Cross
3. Wheeldale Beck
4. A pile of limestone or chippings
5. Jugger Howes Ravine
6. Botton Head 1490 FT
7. 3 and 4
8. Wheeldale Lodge
9. Lyke Wake Stone
10. Bloworth Crossing
11. Section 5 between checkpoints 4 and 5
12. Lilla Howe with Lilla Cross on it
13. Huthwaite green
14. 573033
15. Section 1
16. Grouse
17. Coalmire Plantation

LYKE WAKE TALE

Let me tell you a little tale
Of Brian and his Lyke Wake Trail
Each year we come to hear him talk
All about the Lyke Wake Walk
At the briefing he'll tell you
What you should and shouldn't do
As you walk along the track
With your binliners in your rucksack
According to Brian you'll not fret
For these will stop you getting wet
As on and on you do tread
Don't forgrt to cover your head
For as your told by his mate Pete
This is where you lose most heat
But all in all it's a good day
Friends you'll make along the way
So go along and do your best
You've got the back up from Pete West
And Brian can quell all your fears
He's done the walk the last ten years

                              Geoff Whittaker